ANCIENT ROME
REVEALED

Isabel   Robinson T1

Written by
PETER CHRISP

DK

LONDON, NEW YORK, MUNICH,
MELBOURNE, and DELHI

SENIOR EDITOR SIMON HOLLAND
DESIGNERS JIM GREEN, JOANNE LITTLE,
AND ADRIENNE HUTCHINSON
PHOTOSHOP ILLUSTRATOR LEE GIBBONS
MANAGING EDITOR CAMILLA HALLINAN
MANAGING ART EDITOR SOPHIA TAMPAKOPOULOS
CATEGORY PUBLISHER SUE GRABHAM
ART DIRECTOR MARK RICHARDS
PICTURE RESEARCHER CELIA DEARING
JACKET DESIGNER BOB WARNER
DTP DESIGNER ERIC SHAPLAND
PRODUCTION CONTROLLER DULCIE ROWE

First published in Great Britain in 2003
by Dorling Kindersley Limited,
80 Strand, London WC2R 0RL

2 4 6 8 10 9 7 5 3 1

Copyright © 2003 Dorling Kindersley Limited

A CIP catalogue record for this book
is available from the British Library.

ISBN 0-7513-6820-2

Colour reproduction by
Colourscan, Singapore
Printed in China by
Leo Paper Products

Discover more at
www.dk.com

Hoplomachus
gladiator

CONTENTS

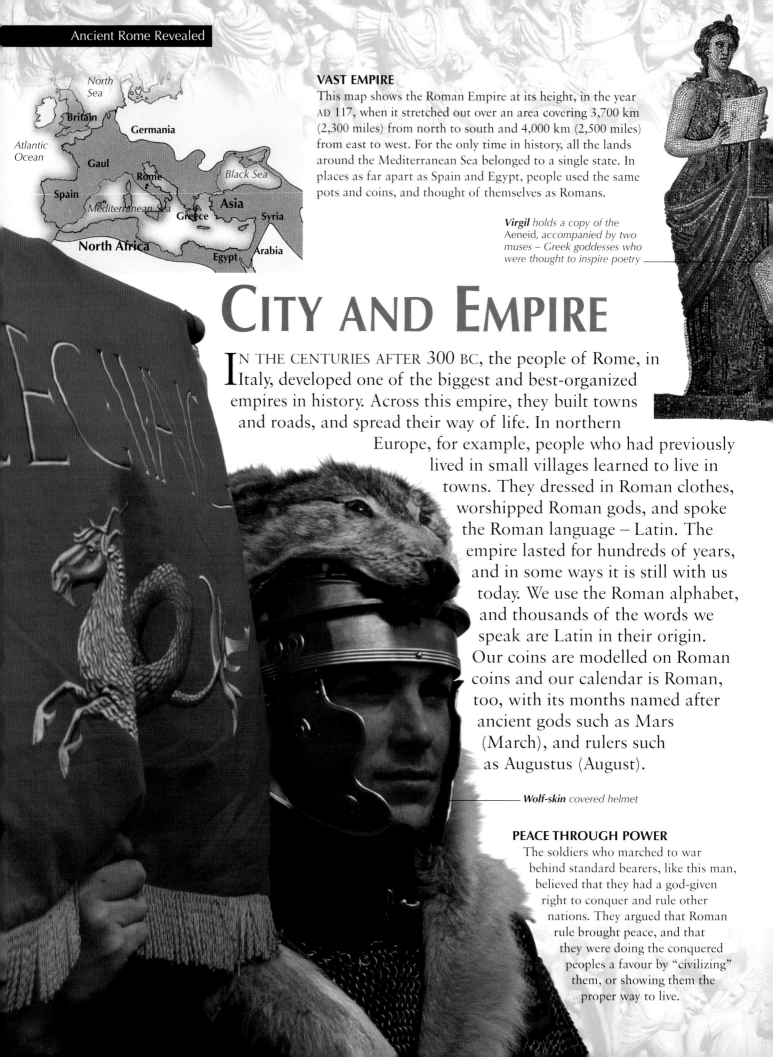

VAST EMPIRE

This map shows the Roman Empire at its height, in the year AD 117, when it stretched out over an area covering 3,700 km (2,300 miles) from north to south and 4,000 km (2,500 miles) from east to west. For the only time in history, all the lands around the Mediterranean Sea belonged to a single state. In places as far apart as Spain and Egypt, people used the same pots and coins, and thought of themselves as Romans.

Virgil holds a copy of the Aeneid, accompanied by two muses – Greek goddesses who were thought to inspire poetry

CITY AND EMPIRE

IN THE CENTURIES AFTER 300 BC, the people of Rome, in Italy, developed one of the biggest and best-organized empires in history. Across this empire, they built towns and roads, and spread their way of life. In northern Europe, for example, people who had previously lived in small villages learned to live in towns. They dressed in Roman clothes, worshipped Roman gods, and spoke the Roman language – Latin. The empire lasted for hundreds of years, and in some ways it is still with us today. We use the Roman alphabet, and thousands of the words we speak are Latin in their origin. Our coins are modelled on Roman coins and our calendar is Roman, too, with its months named after ancient gods such as Mars (March), and rulers such as Augustus (August).

Wolf-skin covered helmet

PEACE THROUGH POWER

The soldiers who marched to war behind standard bearers, like this man, believed that they had a god-given right to conquer and rule other nations. They argued that Roman rule brought peace, and that they were doing the conquered peoples a favour by "civilizing" them, or showing them the proper way to live.

THE ETRUSCANS

The Romans were greatly influenced by the Etruscans, a people whose civilization flourished in central Italy from about the 8th century BC. According to Roman tradition, in the 6th century BC Rome was ruled by Etruscan kings until, around 509 BC, the Romans drove them out and created a republic.

Female head made out of pottery, from an Etruscan tomb

THE GREEK INFLUENCE

Even more important than the Etruscans was the influence of the Greeks, who had founded cities across southern Italy. The Roman poet Virgil modelled his most famous work, the *Aeneid*, on the *Iliad* and *Odyssey*, epic poems by the early Greek writer Homer.

She-wolf suckling (feeding) Romulus and Remus

LEGENDARY ORIGINS

The Romans were so proud of their empire that they believed the gods must have played a part in its beginnings. They invented the story of Romulus and Remus, twin sons of the war god Mars. Abandoned at birth, the twins were brought up by a she-wolf. They decided to create a great city, but disagreed over where to build it. Romulus later killed Remus and named his new city, Rome, after himself.

LANDMARKS OF ROME

1. **Colosseum**, *a huge arena for public shows*

2. **Temple of Claudius**, *an emperor who was declared a god*

3. **Ludus Magnus**, *a training school for gladiators*

4. **Baths of Trajan**, *a vast public bath-house built by Trajan*

5. **Temple of Venus and Rome**, *one of the city's many temples*

6. **Forum of Trajan**, *with monuments to that emperor*

7. **Theatre of Marcellus**, *for plays and concerts*

8. **Temple of Jupiter**, *king of the gods and protector of Rome*

THE CITY OF ROME

This model shows the city of Rome as it looked in the early years of the 4th century AD. To every Roman this was the centre of the world. It was full of great public buildings, such as bath-houses, temples, and theatres, and was home to more than one million people, drawn to the city from many distant lands. What the model does not show are the city's slums, where the poor lived in overcrowded, crumbling blocks of flats.

CAESAR IN GAUL

Julius Caesar shouts, "On, soldiers! The town is ours!" Along the wooden siege rampart, built by the legionaries in 25 days, the men form "tortoises", holding shields above their heads as they rush into the attack. Tall siege towers are wheeled forwards, and the battering rams begin to pound at the walls of Avaricum – the town in Gaul (France) captured by Julius Caesar in 52 BC.

EXPLORING A ROMAN ATTACK

1 **Siege tower:** *a wooden tower on wheels that was rolled up against the Gallic walls*

2 **Battlements:** *fortified towns in Gaul had thick stone walls topped with wooden palisades*

3 **Battering ram:** *wooden beam with an iron head, swung to smash a hole in the wall*

4 **Siege ramp:** *beams and earth were piled up to make an attack platform 24 m (80 ft) high*

5 **Testudo:** *a "tortoise" formation of shields, to protect the advancing legionaries*

6 **Gallic defenders:** *hurled rocks, arrows, hot sand, and flaming torches at the Romans*

7 **Drawbridge:** *lowered from the siege tower, allowing legionaries to storm over the walls*

8 **Final assault with ladders:** *the first man over the wall was given a gold crown, if he lived*

9 **Pilum (javelin):** *the long iron head bent on impact, so that it could not be thrown back*

10 **Chain mail:** *shirts made up of tiny iron rings. Replaced by plate armour in 1st century* AD

NO MORE KINGS

The Romans told many stories about the wickedness of their last king, an Etruscan called Tarquin the Proud. He was so hated that, after he was driven out, the Romans decided that they would never again have a king to rule over them. The republican system was designed to stop any one man from becoming too powerful.

RISE TO POWER

ACCORDING TO ROMAN tradition, Rome was founded in around 753 BC, and was ruled by seven kings. It is certain that by about 366 BC it had become a republic, governed by elected officials called magistrates. The most important were the two consuls, elected each year, who acted as Rome's heads of state and army commanders. They presided over an assembly of ex-magistrates, known as the Senate, which had the power to declare war and create new laws. It was as a republic that Rome rose to power, first gaining control of Italy, and then winning a long series of wars against foreign peoples, such as the Carthaginians of North Africa, the Macedonians who ruled Greece and the Middle East, and the Gauls.

POMPEY THE GREAT

Pompey (106–48 BC) was the Roman general who conquered much of the Middle East, and was given the right to call himself *Magnus* ("the Great"). Pompey was thrilled by this honour, for he modelled himself on the famous Macedonian conqueror King Alexander the Great. In this bust, he even has Alexander's distinctive hair style.

Bronze statue of an Etruscan warrior

HANNIBAL

In 218 BC, a brilliant Carthaginian general called Hannibal invaded Italy with an army that included 37 elephants. Hannibal won several great victories, and spent 16 years roaming Italy. Yet the Romans refused to admit defeat, and eventually won the war.

Hannibal rides a Carthaginian war elephant into Italy. This scene is from an Italian painting of 1508

Roman warship, *powered by oarsmen*

Steering oar

TAKING TO THE SEA

To be able to fight the Carthaginians, who were a great sea power, the Romans had to build their own fleet of ships. Although they knew nothing about naval warfare, they got hold of a stranded Carthaginian warship in 264 BC, and copied it to build their own vessels. The Romans then taught themselves to fight at sea.

Julius Caesar

HUNGRY FOR FAME

Roman politicians such as Pompey and Julius Caesar (c. 100–44 BC) were highly ambitious men who saw victory in war as a means to gaining power, wealth, and lasting fame. They felt that they were in competition – not just with each other, but also with the great men of the past, such as Alexander the Great.

THE CONQUEST OF GAUL

Between 58 and 50 BC, Caesar conquered most of Gaul (France) and led two daring expeditions to Britain. He was so anxious to be remembered for these achievements that he wrote a book about them, entitled *On The Gallic Wars*. We can still read Caesar's books, which are the only surviving accounts of campaigns written by an ancient general.

A stern Roman soldier looks down on a Gallic warrior in this stone relief carving

Replica of a Roman siege works, at Beaune in France

Watch towers, *positioned every 25 m (82 ft) around the edge of the Gallic stronghold*

Stakes, *to prevent the Gauls from climbing the walls*

SIEGE WORKS

Julius Caesar would go to any lengths to win a victory. In order to capture Alesia, a Gallic stronghold, he surrounded it with a massive wooden wall 16 km (10 miles) in length, which had a pair of wide ditches in front of it. Then, Caesar built a second set of defences – behind the first – to protect him and his army in the event of an attack from the rear.

ON THE MARCH

ROMAN FOOT-SOLDIERS, KNOWN AS legionaries, were no braver than most other ancient warriors, such as the Gauls defending Avaricum. The key to Roman success lay in discipline and good organization. New recruits were taught to march in step and to move as a single mass, obeying trumpet signals on a battlefield. Repeated physical exercise, including running and swimming, kept them fit. There were harsh punishments for disobedience or cowardice. Sentries who deserted their posts or fell asleep on duty were beaten to death by their fellow soldiers. There were also rewards for bravery, including military decorations such as the *corona muralis* – the gold crown awarded to the first man over the wall during a siege.

Crest, attached to the helmet for military parades

Legionary's helmet

Cheek guard

A ROMAN LEGION

In the late 1st century AD, there were 28 Roman legions, or armies, each consisting of around 5,500 men. A legion was split into ten divisions, called cohorts, which were also divided into smaller units, called centuries. There were also 120 horsemen, who were the legion's scouts and messengers.

SOLDIER BUILDERS

Legionaries were builders as well as fighters. At the end of a day's march, they had to make a camp, defended by ditches and ramparts topped with wooden stakes. They also built permanent forts out of wood and stone. A Roman fort was like a small town, with streets, a market place, workshops, granaries (for making bread), a hospital, and a bath-house.

Standard

Legionaries building a fort from stone

Centurion

A CENTURY

Each Roman century, containing about 80 men, was commanded by an officer called a *centurion*, who wore a horizontal crest on the top of his helmet. There was also a *cornicen* (trumpeter) and a *signifer* (standard bearer). The standard was seen as a sacred mascot. There was no greater disgrace than letting it fall into enemy hands.

KILLING TOOLS

Going into battle, a legionary took four weapons. He carried two javelins, which he hurled as he charged towards the enemy. For close, hand-to-hand fighting, he drew out his *gladius*, a short sword, used for stabbing rather than slashing at his opponent. If he lost or broke his sword, he had a short emergency dagger, called a *pugio*.

Scabbard (sword sheath), strapped on to the soldier's right-hand side

Pugio, or dagger

Gladius, or short sword

The gaming table was balanced across the knees of the players

14-sided playing or gambling die, with Roman numerals marked on each side

GAMBLING

During their leisure time, off-duty soldiers probably enjoyed board games and gambling. There is even some evidence that they attempted to cheat each other. At the fort of Vindolanda, in northern England, a loaded, six-sided playing die was discovered. It had been weighted so that it would always land on the number six.

DEFENDING THE EMPIRE

As the best soldiers in the Roman army, legionaries were mainly used to conquer foreign countries or squash rebellions. The defence of the empire's borders was left to non-citizen soldiers, known as auxiliaries. Hadrian's Wall, the defensive barrier across northern Britain, was built by legionaries but manned by auxiliaries.

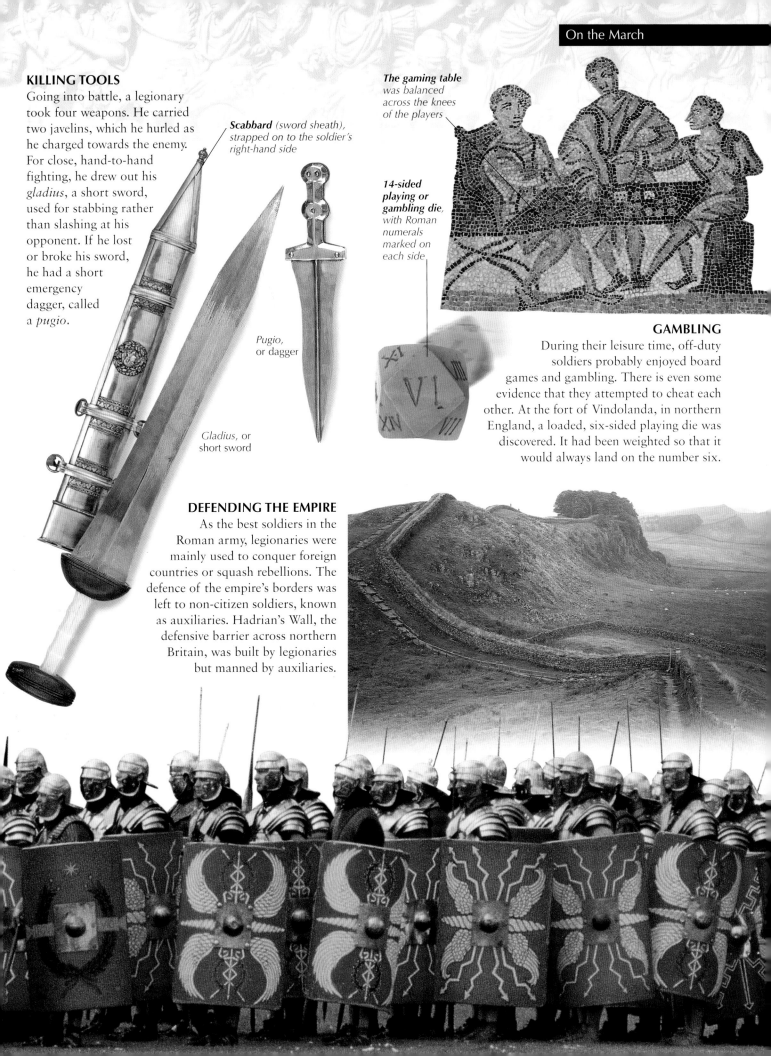

GENERAL SULLA

In 88 BC, Sulla quarrelled with his rival, Marius, over the command of a war in the east. When Marius was chosen to command it instead of him, Sulla marched on Rome, forcing Marius to flee. Sulla was the first Roman general to lead his army on Rome. He set an example that would later be followed by both Julius Caesar and Octavian.

This artwork is an imaginative reconstruction of the conflict between Marius and Sulla. It shows General Sulla leading his army into Rome

REPUBLIC TO EMPIRE

DURING THE 1ST CENTURY BC, there was a series of civil wars. Ambitious Roman politicians fought each other for power, and the republican system was destroyed. The trouble began in 88 BC with a conflict between two rival generals, Marius and Sulla. Then, in 48 BC, Julius Caesar defeated his enemy, Pompey, and made himself dictator – a king in all but name. To save the republic, a group of senators stabbed Caesar to death. Caesar's murder was avenged in a new civil war by his friend, Mark Antony, and adopted son, Octavian. The two then divided the empire between them, only to become enemies themselves. In 31 BC, Octavian defeated Antony in a great sea battle off Actium, in Greece. Octavian, who took the name Augustus, then became Rome's first emperor.

MARK ANTONY

After defeating Caesar's assassins, Mark Antony and Octavian shared the empire between them, with Antony ruling the east and Octavian the west. To make their alliance firmer, Antony married Octavian's sister. Antony then made an enemy of Octavian by abandoning his wife in favour of Cleopatra, the queen of Egypt.

ACTIUM

The Battle of Actium, in which Octavian defeated Antony, brought the civil wars to an end. After his defeat Antony fled to Egypt, where he killed himself. This conflict was such a famous and important event that it was still being painted by artists centuries later. This picture of the battle was painted in 1476–80, by an Italian artist called Neroccio de' Landi.

The actor Rex Harrison as Julius Caesar

Julia, the daughter of Augustus

Senators, wearing wreaths around their heads

The family of Augustus in a procession, as shown on part of the altar's carved frieze

The *Ara Pacis*, or "Altar of Peace"

THE ASSASSINATION OF CAESAR

Julius Caesar's mistake was to act like a king. He even issued coins showing his portrait, an honour that was awarded only to famous Romans after their death. On 15 March 44 BC, he was stabbed to death in the Senate, falling dead at the foot of a statue of his old rival, Pompey. This picture comes from the 1963 film, *Cleopatra*, which re-tells this famous story.

ALTAR OF PEACE

As emperor, Octavian was known as Augustus. After years of civil war, most Romans welcomed the peace brought by Augustus's rule. In Rome, he celebrated the end of the wars by building a great altar dedicated to the goddess Peace. This altar features a carved frieze showing all of his family on a religious procession. This was now the official royal family of Rome.

Rival fleets rammed into each other during the Battle of Actium, and attempted to sink their opponent's ships

Augustus lived to be 75 years old, but his statues always showed him as a young, handsome man

To avoid assassination, Augustus wore a breast-plate underneath his toga

EMPEROR AUGUSTUS

Although he had won power through war, Augustus needed the help of the senators, the leading men of Rome, to run the empire. He claimed to have restored the republic, and made sure that all his actions received the approval of the Senate. In reality, all power lay with him – and this was also true of all the emperors who followed on after him.

COLOSSEUM

STANDING IN THE HEART of Rome is a vast, ruined building called the Colosseum. This was once the ancient world's greatest amphitheatre, an open-air building for public shows. Almost 2,000 years ago, these walls echoed with the deafening cheers of 50,000 spectators. They came to watch beast-hunts, public executions, and above all the gladiators. Armed with swords, nets, and tridents, pairs of gladiators fought fierce duels (single combats), until one was either killed or forced to beg for mercy. If the loser had fought well, the crowd might shout, "Let him live!" If not, their cry would be, "Finish him off!" The final decision of life or death lay with the emperor, watching from the front row.

EXPLORING THE COLOSSEUM

1 **Walls of brick and concrete, lined with stone:** *four viewing tiers (levels) rose to 49 m (160 ft) in height*

2 **Western entrance:** *used by gladiators, who marched in a procession into the arena to begin the show*

3 **Rows of seating:** *Roman senators sat in the front of the first tier, on the same level as the emperor's box*

4 **Underground passages:** *once covered by a wooden floor. Prisoners and animals were kept in cages here*

5 **Masts:** *supported canvas vela ("sails") that sheltered the crowd from the sunshine on hot days*

6 ***Secutor:*** *"pursuer", a gladiator armed with a sword, shield, and manica ("arm guard")*

7 **Helmet:** *this type was egg-shaped and smooth, to avoid being caught in the retiarius's net*

8 ***Retiarius:*** *"net man", who tried to trap the secutor in his net and stab him with his trident*

9 ***Galerus:*** *a metal shoulder-piece protected the neck and head of the retiarius, who had no helmet*

10 ***Lanista:*** *the gladiators' trainer, who acted as a referee or umpire at the fight*

11 **Arena:** *sand-covered fighting area. Arena is the Latin word for "sand", which soaked up the blood and was raked over between fights*

Galerus
(shoulder
guard)

Secutor

Net and
trident

Retiarius

Gladius
(short
sword)

Ocrea – greaves
(leg guards)
made of leather
and bronze

Hoplomachus

Murmillo

THE ENTERTAINERS

The best-known types of gladiator were the *retiarius* and the *secutor*, who were regular opponents in gladiator contests. But there were also several other types. The most heavily armed was the *hoplomachus*, who had leg and arm coverings, a huge helmet, a thrusting spear, and a bowl-shaped shield. The *murmillo* ("fish man") wore a helmet decorated with a fish symbol. He was often pitted against the *retiarius*, or "net man", gladiator.

BREAD AND CIRCUSES

THE POET JUVENAL SAID THAT the people of Rome cared only for two things – bread and circuses. The bread was the monthly distribution of free food, which the emperor gave to every citizen in Rome. The circuses were the courses for chariot racing, just one of many spectacular public shows paid for by the emperor. Other spectacles included theatrical performances, gladiator fights, and mock sea battles, for which amphitheatres were artificially flooded. The people also loved to see wild and exotic animals, brought from distant lands to Rome, where they were killed in the Colosseum or set upon criminals condemned to death. On a smaller scale, similar shows were put on in amphitheatres, racetracks, and theatres all around the empire.

SUPER STADIUMS

The largest and most impressive buildings in Rome were the Circus Maximus – the "great racetrack" – and the Colosseum, whose proper name was the Flavian Amphitheatre, after the family of emperors who planned and built it. The Circus Maximus, enlarged by a long series of Roman politicians and emperors, could hold 255,000 spectators – five times as many people as the Colosseum could contain.

Commodus wearing a
lion-skin headdress, in
the style of Hercules

GLADIATOR EMPEROR

The bloodthirsty Emperor Commodus loved the public shows so much that he became a gladiator himself. In the Colosseum, he fought against gladiators who were armed with blunted weapons, and killed giraffes, ostriches, and tame tigers. Commodus wanted to be seen as another Hercules, the mighty monster-killer from Roman legends.

Emperor watching
from the Colosseum's
imperial box

ANIMAL SHORTAGE

The need for large numbers of wild animals, to supply the Roman amphitheatres, had a terrible effect on wildlife. Over time, it became harder and harder to locate lions, tigers, and other animals. As a result, by the early 5th century AD – when this ivory relief was carved – the most exotic wild beasts available for the Colosseum were bears.

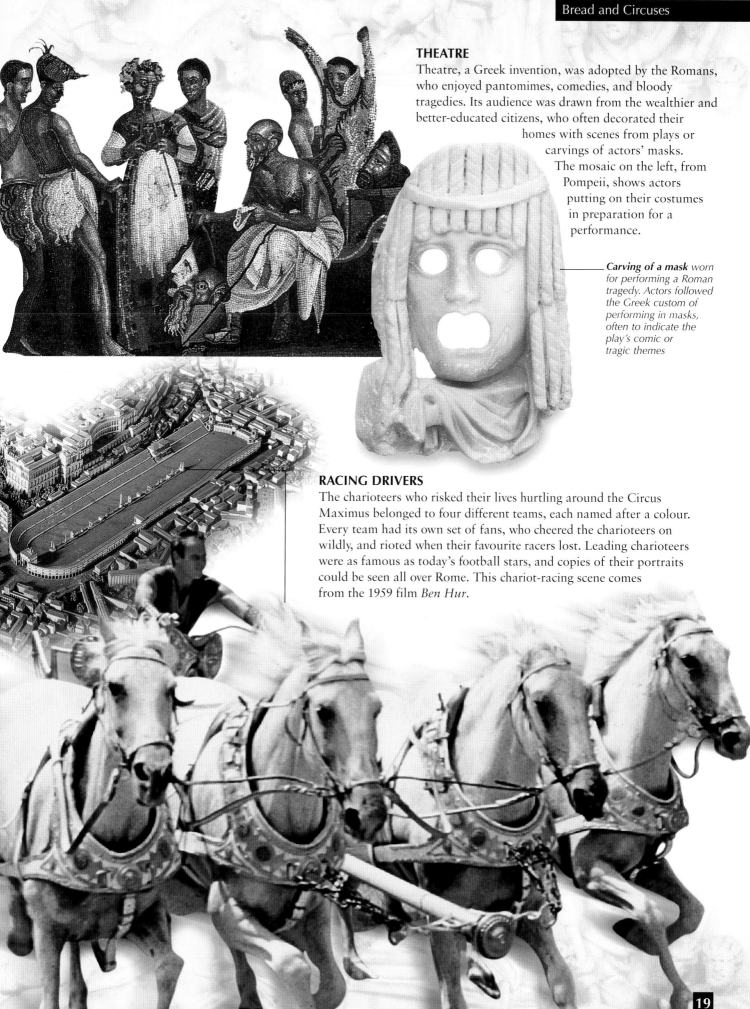

THEATRE

Theatre, a Greek invention, was adopted by the Romans, who enjoyed pantomimes, comedies, and bloody tragedies. Its audience was drawn from the wealthier and better-educated citizens, who often decorated their homes with scenes from plays or carvings of actors' masks.

The mosaic on the left, from Pompeii, shows actors putting on their costumes in preparation for a performance.

Carving of a mask worn for performing a Roman tragedy. Actors followed the Greek custom of performing in masks, often to indicate the play's comic or tragic themes

RACING DRIVERS

The charioteers who risked their lives hurtling around the Circus Maximus belonged to four different teams, each named after a colour. Every team had its own set of fans, who cheered the charioteers on wildly, and rioted when their favourite racers lost. Leading charioteers were as famous as today's football stars, and copies of their portraits could be seen all over Rome. This chariot-racing scene comes from the 1959 film *Ben Hur*.

AQUEDUCTS

This is the 2,000-year-old Pont du Gard (River Gard Bridge) in France. It is part of an aqueduct, a structure for carrying water. The engineers who designed it had to make sure that the water flowed slightly downhill the whole way along its 50-km (31-mile) route from the spring source to the town of Nîmes.

Stone arches *combine to form a light (but strong) structure, ideal for building tiers (levels) in walls and aqueducts*

Pediment

MASTER BUILDERS

THE ROMANS WERE SUCH SKILLED builders that many of their amphitheatres, temples, bridges, and roads are still standing. Two characteristic features of Roman construction are the arch and the use of concrete. A building using arches is as strong as one with solid walls, yet it is much quicker to build. Concrete, a Roman invention, was made up of rubble dropped into a sticky mortar made from lime (burnt chalk or limestone), *pozzolana* (volcanic ash), and water. Different sizes and weights of rubble were used, depending on whether the concrete needed to be light for making ceilings, or strong for making load-bearing walls. Like the arch, concrete allowed the Romans to build vast structures quickly.

— *Temple of Augustus and Livia* at Vienne, in France

These recessed squares were included to make the dome lighter in weight

GREEK DESIGN

The Romans copied Greek architecture, building temples with rows of columns that supported triangular pediments, which were richly decorated with statues. The main difference was this: while Greek temples were constructed with carved stone blocks, the Romans used cheaper, mass-produced brick and concrete. Expensive carved stone was used only for the cladding (outer skin) of the building.

Plumb bob

Chisel Dividers

Set square

TOOLS OF THE TRADE

The Roman engineers who designed aqueducts and temples were highly skilled and well trained. Some of them were so proud of their work that they had the tools of their trade carved on to their tombstones. On this tomb, you can see set squares, for marking right angles, and a plumb bob – a weighted length of string for checking that upright lines were true (straight).

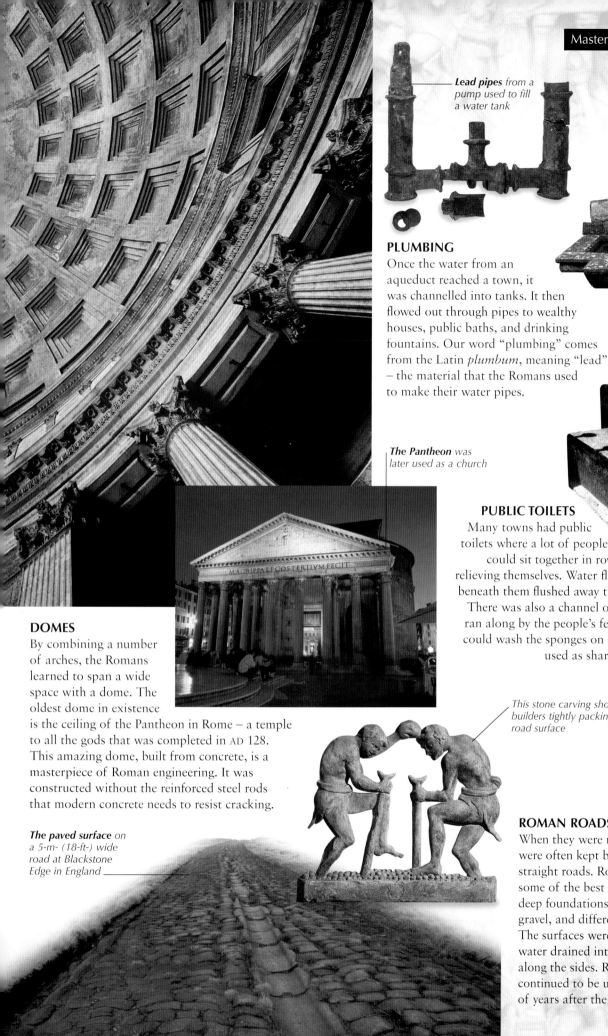

Lead pipes from a pump used to fill a water tank

Roman fountain from Fontfroide, in France – fed by lead pipes

PLUMBING

Once the water from an aqueduct reached a town, it was channelled into tanks. It then flowed out through pipes to wealthy houses, public baths, and drinking fountains. Our word "plumbing" comes from the Latin *plumbum*, meaning "lead" – the material that the Romans used to make their water pipes.

The Pantheon was later used as a church

PUBLIC TOILETS

Many towns had public toilets where a lot of people could sit together in rows, relieving themselves. Water flowing beneath them flushed away the waste. There was also a channel of water that ran along by the people's feet, so that they could wash the sponges on sticks that they used as shared toilet paper.

DOMES

By combining a number of arches, the Romans learned to span a wide space with a dome. The oldest dome in existence is the ceiling of the Pantheon in Rome – a temple to all the gods that was completed in AD 128. This amazing dome, built from concrete, is a masterpiece of Roman engineering. It was constructed without the reinforced steel rods that modern concrete needs to resist cracking.

The paved surface on a 5-m- (18-ft-) wide road at Blackstone Edge in England

This stone carving shows Roman builders tightly packing down a road surface

ROMAN ROADS

When they were not fighting, soldiers were often kept busy building long, straight roads. Roman roads were some of the best ever made. They had deep foundations and layers of sand, gravel, and different-sized stones. The surfaces were curved, so that rain water drained into ditches carved out along the sides. Roman roads continued to be used for thousands of years after the empire fell.

ASHES OF POMPEII

BENEATH THE HOT ITALIAN SUN, early in the 20th century, archaeologists gradually uncover more and more of Pompeii, the scene of one of the worst natural disasters in history. On 24 August in AD 79, Mount Vesuvius, the volcano which towered above Pompeii, erupted – sending up a thick cloud of ash, pumice, and poisonous fumes. It was as if day had turned to night as the deadly cloud rained down on the town. In a few hours, Pompeii was completely buried.

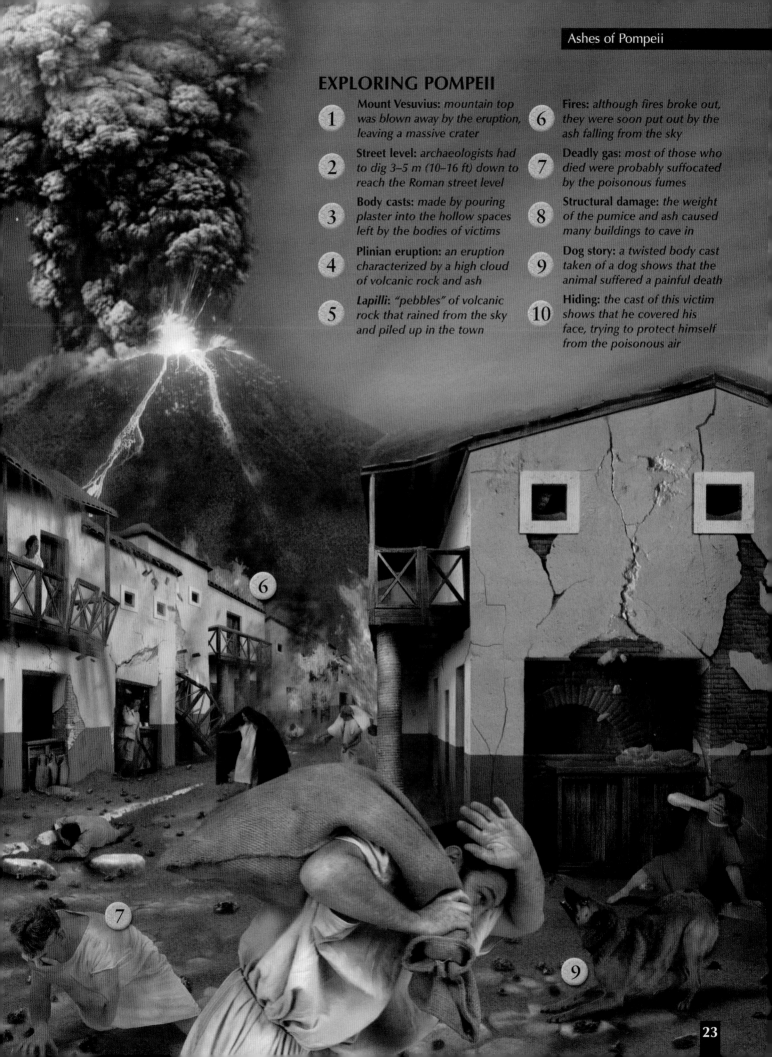

EXPLORING POMPEII

1 Mount Vesuvius: *mountain top was blown away by the eruption, leaving a massive crater*

2 Street level: *archaeologists had to dig 3–5 m (10–16 ft) down to reach the Roman street level*

3 Body casts: *made by pouring plaster into the hollow spaces left by the bodies of victims*

4 Plinian eruption: *an eruption characterized by a high cloud of volcanic rock and ash*

5 Lapilli: *"pebbles" of volcanic rock that rained from the sky and piled up in the town*

6 Fires: *although fires broke out, they were soon put out by the ash falling from the sky*

7 Deadly gas: *most of those who died were probably suffocated by the poisonous fumes*

8 Structural damage: *the weight of the pumice and ash caused many buildings to cave in*

9 Dog story: *a twisted body cast taken of a dog shows that the animal suffered a painful death*

10 Hiding: *the cast of this victim shows that he covered his face, trying to protect himself from the poisonous air*

HERCULANEUM

The town of Herculaneum was Pompeii's neighbour, and was buried under 15–18 m (50–60 ft) of boiling mud after the volcano erupted. Many organic materials were preserved here by a process of partial burning, known as carbonization. These include wooden furniture, the hull of a boat, cloth, loaves of bread left in an oven, and 1,200 scrolls – books from a library that belonged to Julius Caesar's father-in-law.

TIME TRAVELLING

THE TOWN OF POMPEII is just one of thousands of Roman discoveries made by archaeologists. The lands around the Mediterranean Sea are all rich in Roman remains, including towns, forts, villas (country houses), and roads. Marine archaeologists also scour the seabed for ancient shipwrecks. Some of the best finds come from Roman rubbish dumps. In one dump, at the fort of Vindolanda in northern England, archaeologists discovered more than 1,000 letters written on thin wooden tablets. Usually, wood quickly rots in the ground and disappears, but these letters survived thanks to the waterlogged soil. When we read a letter written by an ancient Roman, we can feel the long-dead past come to life again.

One of 300 skeletons found at Herculaneum

SKELETONS

Skeletons such as this one, from Herculaneum, can tell us a lot about the health and lifestyle of the ancient Romans. Bones often show signs of disease and of a good or bad diet. Several skeletons from Herculaneum showed evidence of lead poisoning, which could have been caused by lead cooking pots, water pipes, or lead-based cosmetics (make-up).

ROMAN LETTERS

The Vindolanda tablets include shopping lists, an invitation to a birthday party – and an appeal by a soldier to an officer, in which he begs not to be "beaten with rods". The tablets also give us a rare opportunity to see what Roman handwriting looked like.

Thin leaf of wood, about the size of a modern postcard

UNCOVERED WONDERS

Unlike Roman paintings, mosaics – pictures made from tiny, coloured tiles – can last for thousands of years. Some of the finest examples were found in Herculaneum, including this lovely picture of the sea god, Neptune, and his wife, Salacia – who is better known by her Greek name, Amphitrite. It decorated the wall of an outdoor dining room, used during the summer.

In summertime, diners reclined on three couches arranged around a central pool

Neptune, god of the sea

Salacia, the queen of the sea in Roman mythology

Hypocausts *like this are found all over regions that were once part of the Roman Empire*

CENTRAL HEATING

This is the *caldarium*, or "hot room", of a bath-house at the Roman fort of Chesters in northern England. You can still see that the floor in the room was raised up on stacks of tiles. This raised floor was part of the *hypocaust* heating system. Hot air from a nearby furnace flowed beneath the floor and up through spaces in the walls, provided by hollow "box tiles", to heat the room.

STUDYING A MOSAIC

Every archaeologist digging at a Roman site dreams of uncovering a mosaic. Mosaics are greatly valued – not just for their beauty, but also because of the information they can give us. Experts have identified different schools of mosaicists, who seem to have had their own styles, working methods, and favourite patterns and subjects. The most popular subjects were the changing seasons, wild animals, and scenes from Roman myths.

Archaeologist *preserving a mosaic showing wild animals*

Household slave, as shown in a mosaic from Sicily

WOMEN

Roman women had fewer rights than men. They could not vote in political elections, or follow careers in politics or the law. The Romans strongly believed that a woman's place was in the home, raising children. Even so, women could own property and run their own businesses. Many also played an important public role in religion, as priestesses.

SOCIAL SCENES

THERE WERE DIFFERENT CLASSES in Roman society, each with different rights. The most basic division was between the free and the slaves. A slave was any man, woman, or child who could be bought and sold, and basically treated as property. The free were also split into two groups – citizens, and non-citizens or *peregrini* ("foreigners"). Citizens paid fewer taxes than *peregrini* and had more rights. The citizens themselves also belonged to different classes. At the top was the senatorial order, the ruling class of Rome. Senators commanded legions, governed provinces, and acted as priests. Below them were the equestrians (knights), some of whom worked for the emperor at home and abroad. These were the wealthy classes, and below them was the great mass of ordinary citizens – small-scale farmers, traders, and the legionaries of the Roman army.

HOUSEHOLD SLAVES

Life for slaves varied greatly. It was hardest for the slaves who worked as miners or farm workers, often chained up to stop them running away. Household slaves had a much better life, especially if they belonged to a rich owner. Many were the children of slave parents and grew up feeling as if they were part of their owner's family.

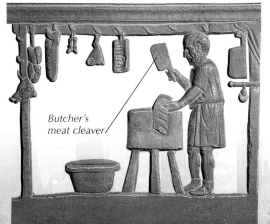

Butcher's meat cleaver

FREEDMEN

Many slaves were able to save up money and buy their freedom, while others were freed as a reward for their loyal service. These freedmen, or ex-slaves, often went into small businesses as shopkeepers. The butcher shown here was a freedman who had become wealthy enough to afford a carved tombstone. The carving shows him hard at work, proud of his trade.

THE SENATE

This is the Forum in Rome – the heart of government, where the senators met for regular meetings in the *Curia*, or Senate House. Under the republic, this was where laws were made and decisions were taken to go to war. Although these powers were taken over by the emperor, the Senate kept hold of its social prestige.

Covered heads, showing these men's status as priests

CITIZENS IN TOGAS

Social rank was displayed by clothing. Only Roman citizens had the right to wear a toga, which was a heavy woollen robe worn in complicated folds. Equestrians showed their status with a narrow purple stripe on their tunic, while senators wore a tunic with a broad purple stripe.

BECOMING A CITIZEN

Non-citizens could become citizens and win the right to wear a toga – like the baker Terentius Neo did, shown here in a portrait with his wife. Another example are the non-citizens who served in the army, in special units called auxiliaries. Auxiliary soldiers were paid less than legionaries, but could become citizens when they retired. Also, Roman citizenship was often given to foreigners as a reward for their services, or to win their loyalty.

Terentius Neo holds a scroll, while his wife (far left) holds a wax tablet and a pointed stylus for writing on it. They may have included such expensive and intellectual materials in their portrait to show off their new status

A taxation scene, taken from a Roman altar

CITIZENSHIP FOR ALL

Over time, the number of citizens increased. Then, in AD 212, the Emperor Caracalla extended citizenship to include every free man in the empire. One theory is that he did this in order to raise more money – for Caracalla had introduced new taxes, which only the citizens had to pay.

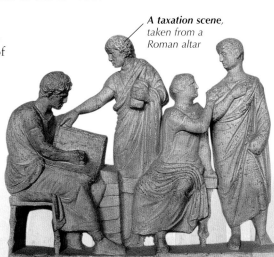

This coin of Emperor Nero celebrates the completion, in
AD 64, of a new harbour for Rome at Ostia, on the mouth
of the River Tiber. It shows Ostia's quays, cargo ships, and a
statue of the sea god, Neptune, on top of a new lighthouse.
Ostia became the main port for Rome's grain supply, most
of which was grown in Sicily and North Africa.

God of the Tiber
watching over the
river's entrance

ROMAN RICHES

ROMAN RULE BROUGHT PEACE to all the lands around
the Mediterranean Sea. This was a great boost to
trade, because it made it easier for merchants to travel from
one land to another with their goods. The Roman navy
hunted down pirates, allowing merchant ships to cross the
Mediterranean without fear of being attacked. Trade was also
aided by the spread of a common language – Latin in the west of
the empire and Greek in the east of the empire. A single currency
was another huge advantage – from Egypt in the south to Britain
in the north, people used the same Roman coins. Roman wealth
also attracted merchants from lands beyond the empire, bringing
silk from China and spices from India and Arabia.

Hold packed with
amphorae *of wine*
and sacks of grain

HARVESTING MACHINE

To increase the grain supply, the Romans invented
a harvesting machine called a *vallum*. This was a
large frame with a toothed edge, mounted on
wheels, which was pushed through a field of corn
so that the cut ears fell into the frame.
This was much quicker than the
usual method of harvesting by
hand using sickles.

Stone relief of a
harvesting scene,
from Gaul (France)

Raising or lowering the
handle adjusted the height
of the cutting edge

Mule – *oxen were also*
used to drive machines

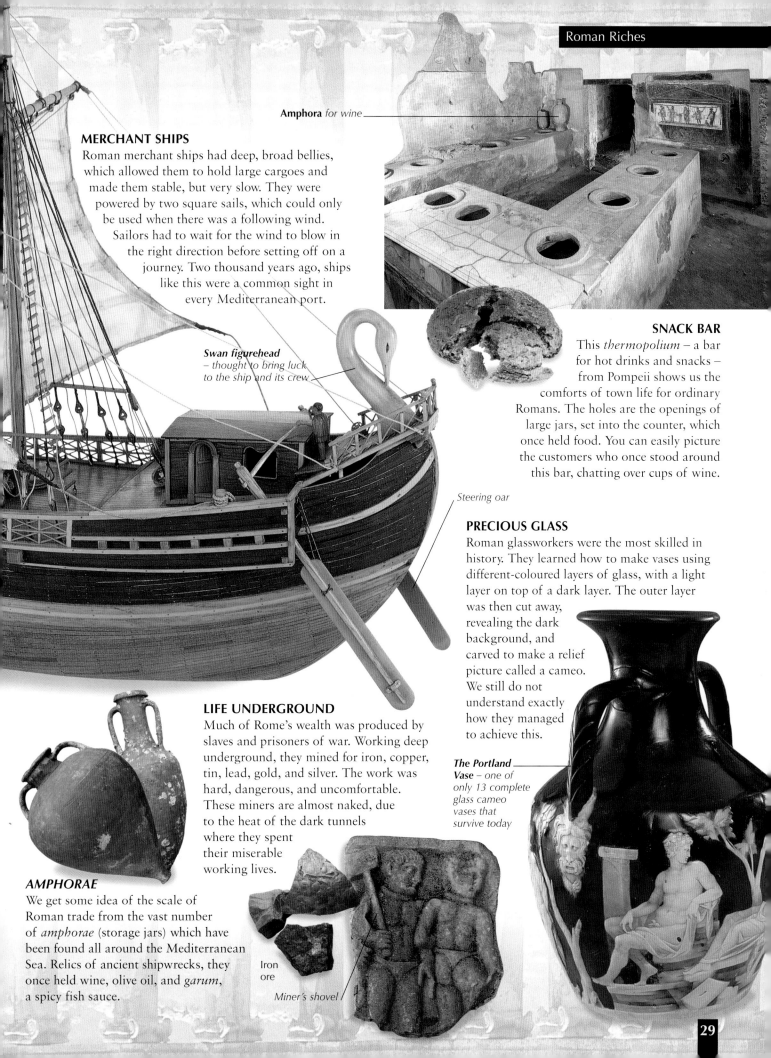

Amphora *for wine*

MERCHANT SHIPS

Roman merchant ships had deep, broad bellies, which allowed them to hold large cargoes and made them stable, but very slow. They were powered by two square sails, which could only be used when there was a following wind. Sailors had to wait for the wind to blow in the right direction before setting off on a journey. Two thousand years ago, ships like this were a common sight in every Mediterranean port.

Swan figurehead
– thought to bring luck to the ship and its crew

SNACK BAR

This *thermopolium* – a bar for hot drinks and snacks – from Pompeii shows us the comforts of town life for ordinary Romans. The holes are the openings of large jars, set into the counter, which once held food. You can easily picture the customers who once stood around this bar, chatting over cups of wine.

Steering oar

PRECIOUS GLASS

Roman glassworkers were the most skilled in history. They learned how to make vases using different-coloured layers of glass, with a light layer on top of a dark layer. The outer layer was then cut away, revealing the dark background, and carved to make a relief picture called a cameo. We still do not understand exactly how they managed to achieve this.

The Portland Vase *– one of only 13 complete glass cameo vases that survive today*

LIFE UNDERGROUND

Much of Rome's wealth was produced by slaves and prisoners of war. Working deep underground, they mined for iron, copper, tin, lead, gold, and silver. The work was hard, dangerous, and uncomfortable. These miners are almost naked, due to the heat of the dark tunnels where they spent their miserable working lives.

AMPHORAE

We get some idea of the scale of Roman trade from the vast number of *amphorae* (storage jars) which have been found all around the Mediterranean Sea. Relics of ancient shipwrecks, they once held wine, olive oil, and *garum*, a spicy fish sauce.

Iron ore

Miner's shovel

HOUSE OF THE FAUN

THE BIGGEST HOUSE in Pompeii is the House of the Faun, named after a statue of a dancing faun found amongst the remains of the *atrium*, or entrance hall, of the building. Its owner was one of the richest and most important men in the town. Every morning, this *atrium* was crowded with visitors, called the owner's clients, who came to pay him their respects and ask for favours. One by one, they were led by a slave to see the owner, known as their patron. In return for his help and protection, the clients gave him support in business or political matters. The more clients a patron had, the greater was his prestige.

EXPLORING A ROMAN *ATRIUM*

1 **House of the Faun:** *this great Roman* domus *(town house) took up an entire* insula *(street block), covering an area of 3,000 sq m (32,000 sq ft)*

2 **Atrium:** *the large entrance hall of a rich Roman house, where guests and clients were greeted*

3 **Peristylium:** *garden court with colonnaded, covered walkways that provided shade on hot days. Beyond this one lies a second, even larger* peristylium

4 **Tablinum:** *the small side room, or office, where the owner of the house – the man sitting on the couch – received his clients and other visitors*

5 **Impluvium:** *ornamental basin filled with rain water that fell through the* compluvium, *an opening in the ceiling that also let light into the room*

6 **The Faun:** *an 80-cm- (31-in-) high bronze statue of a dancing faun, a friendly spirit of the woods and fields*

7 **Clients:** *supporters of the master of the house, who was their patron. They would be smartly dressed when visiting, wearing togas*

8 **Slave:** *a house this size was staffed by dozens of slaves, who cooked, cleaned, waited on their owners, and even helped the master to dress in the morning*

9 **Mural:** *a decorative, patterned frieze – one of many paintings that covered the walls throughout the house*

10 **Mosaic floor:** *these geometric (regular), black and white patterns were made up of thousands of tiny* tesserae *(ceramic tiles)*

GETTING DRESSED
The Romans rose early, at sunrise. A rich woman would spend a long time getting dressed, assisted by female slaves. Her hair was arranged in the latest style, and the slaves applied perfume and make-up. Cosmetics included a mixture of soot and bear fat, used to blacken the eyebrows, and red blusher made from wine dregs.

Wall painting of women at their toilet (dressing table)

Model of an apartment block in the Roman port town of Ostia

LIFE AND LEISURE

THERE WERE BIG DIFFERENCES between the lives of rich and poor Romans. While the wealthy could afford to live luxuriously – in homes like the House of the Faun – the poor often lived in small rooms in apartment blocks, which might be four or five storeys high. Even so, both the rich and the poor could enjoy many of the same pleasures, such as an afternoon visit to an amphitheatre, racetrack, or a bath-house. A public bath-house was an important social centre in every Roman town. At the baths, people from all levels of society washed, relaxed, exercised, and took part in sports such as wrestling. Building vast bath-houses was another way in which emperors kept the people happy.

Palm branch, a prize for winning an athletic game or competition

AT THE BATHS
Men and women relaxed separately in public bath-houses. Often, there would be different areas for men and women – or, if not, the two groups would use the baths at different times. This mosaic, from a private bath in Sicily, shows female athletes in bikini-like costumes. In this scene, they are exercising and taking part in sporting competitions.

DINNER TIME
After visiting the baths, it would be time for dinner, which began in the late afternoon or early evening. At dinner, rich Romans lay on couches, leaning on their left elbows while picking at the food with their fingers. The host was expected to provide his guests with entertainment, such as dancing girls, acrobats, or a reading from a new book.

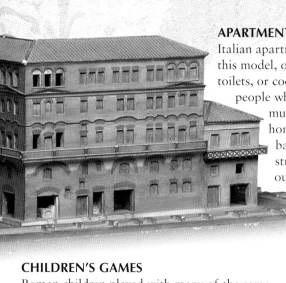

APARTMENT BLOCKS

Italian apartment blocks, like those in this model, often had no running water, toilets, or cooking facilities. The people who lived in them spent much of their time away from home, meeting friends at the baths, taverns, or in the streets. They lived an outdoor lifestyle, just as Mediterranean people still do today.

The hunter thrusts a spear into the boar's chest

CHILDREN'S GAMES

Roman children played with many of the same sorts of toys as children do today, including balls, dolls, pull-along animals, hoops, and glass marbles. With little or no medicine, the death of young children from disease was a common occurrence. Grieving parents often buried children along with their favourite toys and games, which is how we have found out about them.

Pull-along toy horse with wheels

Marbles of coloured glass

HUNTING

Rich men loved to go into the countryside to hunt wild animals, such as stags, wild boars, hares, and foxes. Boar hunting was a dangerous sport, as this mosaic scene shows. The hunters are rescuing the man on the ground, who has just been wounded by the boar's tusks. The mosaic is from the remains of a luxurious Roman palace in Sicily.

GARDENS

A Roman garden was a place to enjoy peace, bird song, and the beauty and perfume of flowers. The poor, who did not have their own, could stroll in the public gardens of bath-houses. We know a lot about Roman gardens, thanks to surviving books on gardening. Archaeologists also study traces left by ancient plant roots, which reveal the patterns of planting and the different varieties grown.

Peristyle garden, recreated among the ruins of a town house in Herculaneum

Wall painting from the 1st century BC

HOUSEHOLD GODS
At the household shrine, statuettes of the gods who protected the home and family were offered daily prayers and gifts of food and wine. This shrine, from a house in Pompeii, contains images of male ancestors. Still seen as important family members, these were honoured alongside the household gods.

DIANA AND ARTEMIS
Roman religion was greatly influenced by Greek gods and myths. The Romans identified Diana, their ancient moon goddess, with the Greek Artemis, goddess of hunting, the moon, and childbirth. So in Roman religion, Diana took on all of Artemis's roles. Roman women giving birth prayed to Diana for a safe delivery of the baby.

Diana holds a bow and arrow, in her role as a huntress. The pains of childbirth were said to be caused by Diana's arrows

ROMAN RELIGION

THE ROMANS WORSHIPPED MANY different gods, who watched over different areas of life. The most powerful was Jupiter, the sky god and special protector of the Roman Empire. Jupiter's statue stood in a great temple on top of Rome's Capitoline Hill. In his role as *Pontifex Maximus* (chief priest) of Rome, the emperor performed ceremonies in honour of many gods. These included prayers, the burning of incense, and sacrifice – the killing of an animal which was offered as a gift to the god. Similar ceremonies took place, on a smaller scale, in every Roman house. Each Roman family was believed to be protected by household gods, whose statuettes were kept in a shrine – a miniature temple in the home.

Oceanus, god of the ocean – thought of as a mighty river flowing around the Earth

White bulls were always sacrificed to Jupiter

This god was often depicted with a serpent – either to show that he was wound around the Earth, like a snake, or because a winding snake reminded the Romans of rivers

TEMPLE WORSHIP
Ceremonies usually took place in front of temples, built as homes to the gods. This carving shows Emperor Marcus Aurelius overseeing the sacrifice of a bull in front of Jupiter's temple, in Rome. Before the bull was killed, the emperor burned incense while reciting the following prayer: "Increase the power of the citizens, the people of Rome, in war and peace".

Statuette of Diana, the huntress, holding her hunter's bow

SMOKY GIFTS

Offerings were usually burned, so that the rising smoke could carry them from this world to the world of the gods. In this 4th-century mosaic, hunters are burning food or incense on an altar, in front of a small statue of Diana. In return for this offering, the men hope that the goddess will assist them in the success of their hunting.

Altar, with charcoal burning on top

Statue of Mithras, wearing his distinctive Persian cap

NEW GODS

As the empire grew, the Romans came across many new gods – most of whom were welcomed into their religion. One newcomer, who was especially popular among soldiers and merchants, was Mithras. His name came from Persia, which was in the eastern part of the empire. He is always depicted killing a bull, with a dog and a snake licking up the flowing blood.

A WORLD FULL OF GODS

The Romans believed that there were gods or spirits everywhere. The entrance to a house was watched over by three separate gods – Forculus, who protected the doors; Limentinus, who guarded the threshold (door sill); and Cardea, goddess of the door hinges. Every river had its own god, shown in Roman art as a bearded man. Before travelling on a river, Romans often prayed to its god for a safe passage.

In this statue, Oceanus is shown holding a steering oar from a Roman ship

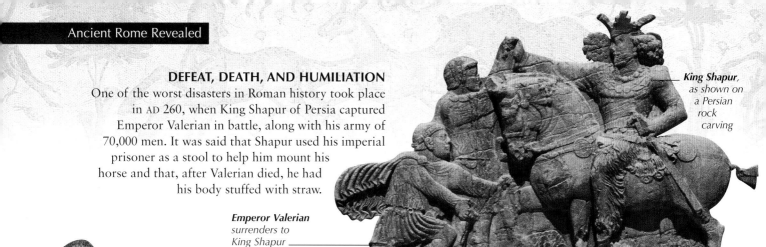

DEFEAT, DEATH, AND HUMILIATION

One of the worst disasters in Roman history took place in AD 260, when King Shapur of Persia captured Emperor Valerian in battle, along with his army of 70,000 men. It was said that Shapur used his imperial prisoner as a stool to help him mount his horse and that, after Valerian died, he had his body stuffed with straw.

King Shapur, as shown on a Persian rock carving

Emperor Valerian surrenders to King Shapur

TIMES OF CHANGE

IN THE 3RD CENTURY THE EMPIRE came under pressure on many sides, with attacks from the Goths in the north and the Sasanian Persians in the east. Frequent defeats, combined with plague and civil wars, led to a rapid turnover of emperors – more than 20 between AD 235 and AD 284 – and breakaway empires in Gaul and in the east. Then, under strong emperors such as Diocletian and Constantine, the empire recovered, and the 4th century was one of great achievement. But, for defence, the Romans relied increasingly on barbarian soldiers, whose people eventually took over the western parts of the empire. The eastern empire lasted for another thousand years.

Eagle-hilted swords – the eagle was the emblem of Rome

VANDALISM

We still use the term "vandal" to refer to someone who destroys something mindlessly. Yet the Vandals, who gave us this word, did not want to destroy the Roman Empire. They simply wanted to share in its wealth. After sweeping through western Europe, they conquered North Africa. Here, they imitated the lifestyle of the Romans, living in villas decorated with mosaics. This mosaic shows a Vandal on horseback in Roman-style dress. The only "barbarian" feature of his appearance is the long hair.

FOUR EMPERORS

Towards the end of the disastrous 3rd century, the Roman Empire recovered, thanks to a ruler called Diocletian (who was in power from AD 284 to AD 305). Recognizing that the empire was too vast for one emperor to control, Diocletian appointed three co-rulers to share his political burden. This statue shows the tetrarchs ("four rulers") gripping their swords and holding on to each other in a show of united strength.

A later Roman mosaic of Constantine, who was in fact clean-shaven

CHRISTIANITY

Constantine, who was emperor from AD 312 to AD 337, transformed the religion of the empire through his support for Christianity. Christians worshipped only one God, and they had been ill-treated by earlier emperors who thought that they would upset Rome's relationship with its own gods. Constantine, and the emperors after him, encouraged Christian leaders and provided money for churches, so that – gradually – Christianity became the religion of the empire.

Jesus Christ in a Roman toga, with a halo

THE ROMAN CHRIST

As Christianity became the official religion of the late Roman Empire, it took on many features of earlier Roman modes of worship. Instead of praying to different gods for help, people now prayed to Christian saints. In art, Jesus Christ was shown wearing a halo, previously a sign of the Roman sun god. Christ's birthday was also celebrated on the same day as the sun god's – on 25 December.

THE WESTERN LEGACY

In the 5th century AD, the western half of the empire was overrun by Germanic tribes, who then set up their own kingdoms. However, the legacy of Rome was kept alive by the Christian Church, which continued to use the Latin language. The head of the Catholic Church, the Pope, is still known as the *Pontifex Maximus*, an old Roman title meaning "chief priest".

Haghia Sophia, built by Emperor Justinian in AD 532–7

Turkish minaret (mosque tower), used to call the Muslim faithful to prayer

Latin Bible of the 8th century AD, from Hereford in England

THE BYZANTINE EMPIRE

Although the western half of the empire broke up, the eastern half survived for another one thousand years. We now call this the Byzantine Empire – after "Byzantium", an old name for its capital, Constantinople. The eastern empire finally fell in AD 1453, when the Turks captured Constantinople and renamed it Istanbul. The Turks converted the great Roman church of Haghia Sophia into a mosque, a place of worship for Muslim people. This is one of the many cultural examples of how the Roman legacy lives on in the city.

INDEX

ACKNOWLEDGEMENTS

Dorling Kindersley would like to thank:
The Britannia re-enactment group (www.durolitum.co.uk) for participating in the Colosseum and Pompeii photo shoots, and the Colchester Roman Society (www.romanauxilia.com/crswebsite/index.htm), plus DK's Mark Dennis and Archie Clapton for participating in the Avaricum siege and Roman villa photo shoots, Andy Crawford for Avaricum siege and Roman villa photography, Gary Ombler for Colosseum and Pompeii photography, Dorothy Frame for the index, Alyson Lacewing for proof reading, and Sarah Mills for DK Picture Library research.

The publisher would like to thank the following for their kind permission to reproduce their photographs:
Key: a = above; b = below; c = centre; l = left; r = right; t = top; ace=acetate

Ancient Art & Architecture Collection: 36cl; Mike Andrews 7cr, 11b; R. Ashworth 27tl; Dr. S. Coyne 16-16ace, 17tr, 35tl; L. Ellison 13cbr; Leslie Ellison 25cr; G. T. Garvey 29bcr; Brian Gibbs 5tr, 12-13b; D. J. Justice 26tl; Ronald Sheridan 11cr, 13tr, 19tl, 20-21tc, 25tr, 26bl, 27tr, 28b, 34-35, 37tr, 37br; John Stevens 18-19c; B. Wilson 28tl; Julian Worker 36tr. **Ashmolean Museum:** 10l. **Richard Ashworth:** 24-25c. **Bridgeman Art Library, London / New York:** 29tr; Guildhall Art Gallery, Corporation of London 32bl; Laurus 37tl; Museo Archeologico Nazionale, Naples 10-11tc, 34tl; Museo della Civilta Romana, Rome 21bcr; Museo Etrusco di Villa Giulia / Alinari 7tr; Musée du Louvre, Paris 27br. **British Museum:** 19tr, 20br, 20cbr, 21tc, 24br, 29bl, 33cl, 35cr. **Corbis:** 14-15tc, 23-23tc ace; Paul Almasy 21tr; Archivio Iconografico, S.A. 15tr, 26tr, 34bl; Yann Arthus-Bertrand 37cl; Bettmann 14tl, 14c, 15br; Jonathan Blair 24tr, 24cl; Burstein Collection 10cr; Robert

Estall 21bl; John Heseltine 22-22b ace; Mimmo Jodice 32tl, 34tr; David Lees 20bl; Charles & Josette Lenars 6bl; Araldo de Luca 5cr, 6-7t&b, 7bl, 10-11t&b, 12-13t&b, 14-15t&b, 18bl, 26-27b, 32-33tc, 33cr; Lance Nelson 21cl; North Carolina Museum of Art 14-15b; Gianni Dagli Orti 10b; Ricki Rosen / Saba 25bl; Leonard de Selva 32cr; Sean Sexton Collection 22-22br ace; Paul Thompson / Eye Ubiquitous 17-17ace; Gian Berto Vanni 30-30ace, 31-31bc ace; Ruggero Vanni 20cl; Vanni Archive 15cr; Roger Wood 5bl, 6-7tc, 33b; Adam Woolfitt 29br. **Alistair Duncan:** 3t&b, 4-5t&b, 24-25t&b, 26-27t&b, 28-29t&b, 32-33t&b, 34-35t&b, 36-37t&b, 38t&b. **Ermine Street Guard:** 12cl. **Gables:** 22br. **Getty Images:** Hulton Archive 22tc, 22-22 cl ace, 22-22cr ace; Raymond Kleboe / Hulton Archive 22-22bl ace, 22bcl. **John Heseltine:** 2, 12cr, 36br, 39. **Simon James:** 11tr, 18-19t&b, 20-21t&b. **Museo Archeologico Di Napoli:** 22bl. **National Maritime Museum:** 28-29tc. **The Picture Desk:** The Art Archive / Musée du Louvre Paris / Dagli Orti 18br; The Kobal

Collection / MGM 19b. **Scala Group S.p.A.:** Chieto, Museo Nazionale, © 1990, courtesy of the Ministero Beni e Att. Culturali 31-31tc Ace; Naples, Museo Nazionale © 1990, courtesy of the Ministero Beni e Att. Culturali 31bl Ace. **Karl Shone:** 12tl. **University Museum of Newcastle:** 13tcl. **Werner Forman Archive:** 33tr. **Lin White:** 21cr, 22-22t Ace, 23cr. **Alan Williams:** 5cl, 20tl.

Jacket credits – Front: Ancient Art and Architecture Collection: Dr. S. Coyne l. **Back: Corbis:** Archivio Iconografico, S. A. tr. **Spine: Corbis:** Archivio Iconografico, SA.

All other images © Dorling Kindersley. For further imformation, see: www.dkimages.com

Every effort has been made to trace copyright holders of photographs. The publishers apologize for any omissions.